TEAM SPIRIT®

SMART BOOKS FOR YOUNG FANS

THE MINNESOTA VIKINGS

BY
MARK STEWART

NORWOODHOUSE PRESS

CHICAGO, ILLINOIS

Norwood House Press
P.O. Box 316598
Chicago, Illinois 60631

For information regarding Norwood House Press, please visit our website at:
www.norwoodhousepress.com or call 866-565-2900.

All photos courtesy of Getty Images except the following:
Icon SMI (4), Author's Collection (7, 15, 33, 35 bottom),
Topps, Inc. (9, 16, 17, 20, 21, 34 both, 35 top right, 37, 38, 43 both, 45),
Black Book Partners (10, 23, 28, 39, 40), SportsChrome (14), McDonald's Corp. (35 top left),
Hostess Brands (42 top), Harris Publications, Inc. (42 bottom), Matt Richman (48).
Cover Photo: Icon SMI

The memorabilia and artifacts pictured in this book are presented for educational and informational purposes,
and come from the collection of the author.

Editor: Mike Kennedy
Designer: Ron Jaffe
Project Management: Black Book Partners, LLC.
Special thanks to Topps, Inc.

Library of Congress Cataloging-in-Publication Data

Stewart, Mark, 1960-
  The Minnesota Vikings / by Mark Stewart.
      p. cm. -- (Team spirit)
  Includes bibliographical references and index.
  Summary: "A revised Team Spirit Football edition featuring the Minnesota
Vikings that chronicles the history and accomplishments of the team.
Includes access to the Team Spirit website which provides additional
information and photos"--Provided by publisher.
  ISBN 978-1-59953-529-6 (library edition : alk. paper) -- ISBN
978-1-60357-471-6 (ebook) 1. Minnesota Vikings (Football
team)--History--Juvenile literature. I. Title.
  GV956.M5S74 2012
  796.332'6409776579--dc23
                                                        2012018799

Manufactured in the United States of America in North Mankato, Minnesota.
205N—082012

COVER PHOTO: The Vikings celebrate a touchdown during the 2010 season.

Table of Contents

ABOUT OUR GLOSSARY

In this book, there may be several words that you are reading for the first time. Some are sports words, some are new vocabulary words, and some are familiar words that are used in an unusual way. All of these words are defined on page 46. Throughout the book, sports words appear in **bold type**. Regular vocabulary words appear in ***bold italic type***.

Meet the Vikings

Purple is a color that is familiar to anyone who plays football. That's because bumps and bruises are part of the game. The Minnesota Vikings take purple to a whole new level. They have made it one of the most famous colors in sports. The Vikings don't just wear purple—they live it. No team tackles more ferociously or blocks with more power.

All that hard work gives Vikings fans something to cheer about in every game. Just as important, it gives Minnesota's stars a chance to show off their skill and creativity. The Vikings may be known for playing physical football, but they have also had some of the most exciting and graceful players ever.

This book tells the story of the Vikings. In some seasons, they have had an unstoppable offense. In others, their defense has taken control. When the Vikings put both together at the same time, they are one of the most remarkable teams in football.

Percy Harvin gets a hug after scoring a touchdown. The Vikings have always been able to find exciting and graceful players.

Glory Days

The 1960s were a great *decade* for sports in Minnesota. During this *era*, the state welcomed *professional* teams in baseball, hockey, and basketball. Pro football also took hold in Minnesota. The first team was supposed to begin play in 1960 as part of the newly formed **American Football League (AFL)**. However, at the last moment, the new team's owners decided to join the **National Football League (NFL)** instead. That is how the Vikings were born. Minnesota played its first season in 1961 and made headlines by beating the Chicago Bears—one of the NFL's best teams—on opening day.

In their early years, the Vikings built their team around a handful of young stars, including quarterback Fran Tarkenton, running back Tommy Mason, and defensive lineman Jim Marshall. By the

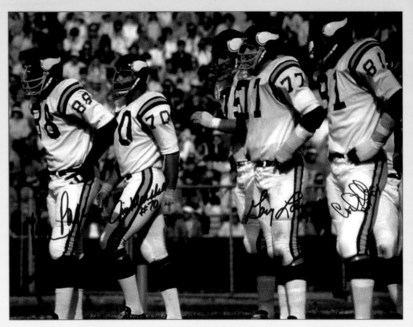

late 1960s, Minnesota was ready to challenge for the NFL championship. The offense was led by running backs Bill Brown and Dave Osborn, kicker Fred Cox, and lineman Ron Yary. Meanwhile, Joe Kapp replaced Tarkenton as the team's quarterback. Kapp had been the **Most Valuable Player (MVP)** in the **Canadian Football League (CFL)**.

The Vikings were best known for their defense. Marshall, Gary Larsen, Carl Eller, and Alan Page made up a defensive line nicknamed the "Purple People Eaters." Other stars included defensive backs Bobby Bryant and Paul Krause. The Vikings won the NFL championship in 1969.

The coach of that team was Bud Grant. He would lead the Vikings for 18 seasons in all. Grant was tough and smart. He taught the Vikings to play the same way. During the 1970s, Grant built Minnesota into a powerhouse. His quarterback was Tarkenton, who returned to the team in 1972.

LEFT: Fran Tarkenton looks for an open teammate.
ABOVE: All four Purple People Eaters signed this souvenir photo.

7

Tarkenton guided a high-scoring offense that also featured a great running back named Chuck Foreman. He made a big impact as a **rookie** in 1973 and retired as the team's all-time leading rusher. Minnesota also had a talented group of receivers, including John Gilliam, Ahmad Rashad, and Sammy White.

Minnesota played in the **Super Bowl** three times during the 1970s. Unfortunately, they could not win the title. In the 1980s, the Vikings moved to an indoor stadium and remade their team with fast, exciting players such as Anthony Carter, Cris Carter, Jake Reed, and Herschel Walker. They also had several good quarterbacks, including Tommy Kramer, Rich Gannon, and Warren Moon.

In 1998, the Vikings had an incredible season with a 15–1 record. John Randle and Ed McDaniel were the stars of a hard-hitting defense. Quarterback Randall Cunningham led the club's passing attack. His favorite receivers were Cris Carter and Randy Moss, who scored 17 touchdowns. Robert Smith ran through holes opened by Randall McDaniel and Todd Steussie. Kicker Gary Anderson set an NFL record with 164 points. The Vikings advanced to the championship game of the **National Football Conference (NFC)**.

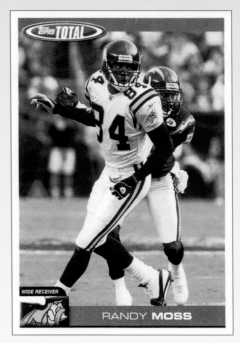

LEFT: Quarterback Brett Favre is in the middle of a Viking sandwich, courtesy of John Randle and Fernando Smith.   **ABOVE**: This trading card shows how closely opponents needed to cover Randy Moss.

They hosted the Atlanta Falcons and suffered a painful loss in **overtime**.

As the 21st century began, the recipe for success in Minnesota was still the same. The offense relied on Adrian Peterson, an explosive rusher who thrilled fans with his long touchdown runs. Receivers Sidney Rice, Bernard Berrian, and Percy Harvin gave Minnesota major weapons in the passing game. Matt Birk and Steve Hutchinson *anchored* the offensive line. The Vikings built their new club around talented defensive players such as Kevin Williams, Pat Williams, Antoine Winfield, Chad Greenway, and Jared Allen.

The only thing missing was a star quarterback. The Vikings tried several different passers, including Brad Johnson and Daunte Culpepper. Johnson provided steady leadership, and Culpepper made the **Pro Bowl** three times. But neither could produce a championship. In 2009, Minnesota signed Brett Favre, a legendary quarterback who had won the Super Bowl with the Green Bay Packers.

Favre turned 40 during his first year in Minnesota, but he played

with incredible energy and passion. The Vikings went 12–4 in 2009. Peterson enjoyed his second **All-Pro** season, and Allen had 14.5 **sacks**. The team looked ready to return to the Super Bowl, but an overtime loss in the **playoffs** sent Minnesota home earlier than the fans hoped.

In 2011, the Vikings turned to rookie quarterback Christian Ponder. On his very first pass, Ponder connected with Michael Jenkins on a 72-yard play. Two weeks later, he earned his first victory as a pro. Ponder showed the talent and leadership the Vikings have always looked for in a quarterback. Minnesota fans couldn't help but dream of their first Super Bowl championship.

LEFT: Jared Allen battles to get to the quarterback.
ABOVE: Adrian Peterson breaks free for a big gain.

The Vikings spent their first 21 seasons in Metropolitan Stadium, in the city of Bloomington. The stadium got very cold in the winter—for the fans and the players. The Vikings enjoyed the weather. They used it as part of their home-field advantage.

In 1982, the Vikings opened the Hubert H. Humphrey Metrodome in downtown Minneapolis. The Metrodome was always warm and comfortable, though opponents didn't like it much. It was very hard to hear when the fans stood and cheered. In 2012, the Vikings began making plans with the city of Minneapolis to build a new stadium.

BY THE NUMBERS

- The Vikings' stadium has 64,121 seats.
- The stadium's roof weighs nearly 600,000 pounds.
- After a bad winter storm in 2010, the roof had to be replaced at a cost of $18 million.

When the fans screamed for the Vikings in the Metrodome, it was almost impossible for opponents to hear each other.

Dressed for Success

Unlike most teams, the Vikings represent an entire state instead of a city. They play their games in Minneapolis—which is known as one of the "Twin Cities" along with St. Paul—but they call all of Minnesota their home. Their *logo* shows a Viking's head. The team's name honors the Viking warriors of Scandinavia. Many people in Minnesota are descended from Scandinavians.

Minnesota's colors have been purple, white, and gold since the team's first season in 1961. Today, the Vikings like to wear purple jerseys for home games and all-white uniforms for games on the road. The team's helmet is also purple, with horns on the sides that are meant to honor the ancient Vikings.

LEFT: Christian Ponder models the team's road uniform.
ABOVE: Paul Krause wears the Minnesota home uniform from the 1960s.

We Won!

DAVE OSBORN — **RUNNING BACK**
VIKINGS

Today, winning a championship in the NFL takes two steps. First, a team has to win its conference. Then it has to win the Super Bowl. The Vikings were NFC champions three times, in 1973, 1974, and 1976. Unfortunately, they lost in the Super Bowl each season.

Back in the 1960s, the NFL worked differently. From 1960 to 1965, there was no Super Bowl. The NFL champion stood alone. Starting in the 1966 season, the NFL champion went on to play the AFL champion in the Super Bowl. Win or lose, the NFL champion was still considered the "champion" of the NFL. In 1970, after the two leagues joined forces, the Super Bowl became the official NFL championship. So, the 1969 season would be the last ever for the **NFL Championship Game**. The Vikings made sure it was memorable.

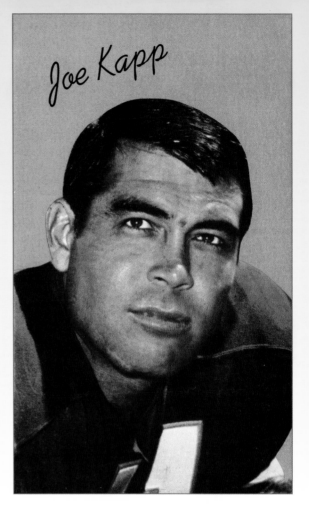

Joe Kapp

Minnesota went 12–2 and finished first in the **Western Conference**. Quarterback Joe Kapp had a great year with 19 touchdown passes. Gene Washington caught nine of them and averaged more than 20 yards per reception. Dave Osborn and Bill Brown shared the rushing duties.

On defense, the Vikings made life miserable for opponents. Jim Marshall and Alan Page put constant pressure on the quarterback. Linebackers Roy Winston and Lonnie Warwick roamed all over the field. Bobby Bryant and Paul Krause were the leaders of a talented **secondary**.

Minnesota rolled into the playoffs against the Los Angeles Rams. Kapp did it all on offense. He passed for 196 yards and led the team in rushing with 42 yards. With the Rams leading 20–14 late in the game, Kapp barreled into the end zone to tie the score. Fred Cox

kicked the **extra point** to give Minnesota the lead. A short time later, Carl Eller sacked Los Angeles quarterback Roman Gabriel for a **safety**. The Vikings won 23–20.

Minnesota hosted the Cleveland Browns for the NFL championship. The game was played on a cold wintry day. The temperature dropped far below freezing, with snow piled up around the field—perfect weather for the Vikings! Early in the first quarter, Kapp smashed through several tacklers and crossed the goal line for a touchdown. The next time the Vikings had the ball, he threw a 75-yard scoring strike to Washington. Minnesota led 14–0.

That was all the scoring the Minnesota defense needed. Cleveland's offense was helpless against the Vikings. Eller, Marshall, Page, and Gary Larsen controlled the **line of scrimmage**. Winston and Wally Hilgenberg chased the Browns all over the field.

In the second half, the Vikings ran the ball against Cleveland at will. Osborn, who gained 108 yards during the game, scored a touchdown to make it 21–0. In the third quarter, Kapp dropped back to pass but was forced to run. He found himself face-to-face with Cleveland's best linebacker, 240-pound Jim Houston. The two collided at top speed and then dropped to the turf. Kapp popped right up and returned to the huddle. A groggy Houston had to be helped to his feet.

The play gave the Vikings an extra spark to finish the game. They won easily, 27–7. Minnesota captured the last NFL championship before a new era of professional football began.

LEFT: Roy Winston tackles Leroy Kelly of the Cleveland Browns.
ABOVE: Jim Marshall, Carl Eller, and Alan Page take a breather during the 1969 playoffs.

Go-To Guys

T o be a true star in the NFL, you need more than fast feet and a big body. You have to be a "go-to guy"—someone the coach wants on the field at the end of a big game. Vikings fans have had a lot to cheer about over the years, including these great stars …

THE PIONEERS

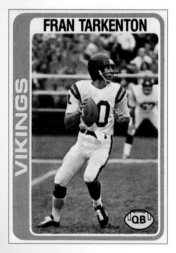

FRAN TARKENTON   Quarterback

- BORN: 2/3/1940
- PLAYED FOR TEAM: 1961 TO 1966 & 1972 TO 1978

Fran Tarkenton loved to scramble when he dropped back to pass. This gave his receivers extra time to get open, and it drove opponents crazy. Tarkenton led the Vikings to the Super Bowl three times. He held the NFL records for passing yards, completions, and touchdowns when he retired.

CARL ELLER   Defensive Lineman

- BORN: 1/25/1942 • PLAYED FOR TEAM: 1964 TO 1978

Carl Eller starred at left defensive end for the Vikings for 15 seasons. He could take down powerful running backs and chase down quarterbacks for a sack. Eller was also an expert at causing a **fumble** and recovering it.

ALAN PAGE Defensive Lineman

- BORN: 8/7/1945 • PLAYED FOR TEAM: 1967 TO 1978

Alan Page was so strong and fast that it was almost impossible to block him. In 1971, the Vikings began keeping track of the number of times he forced opposing quarterbacks into making bad passes. Today, every team in the NFL uses this statistic, known as "hurries."

PAUL KRAUSE Defensive Back

- BORN: 2/19/1942 • PLAYED FOR TEAM: 1968 TO 1979

Paul Krause was the perfect safety for Minnesota's great defenses of the 1960s and 1970s. When opposing quarterbacks panicked and threw without looking, he was there to **intercept** the pass. Krause retired with 81 interceptions, more than anyone in history.

RON YARY Offensive Lineman

- BORN: 7/16/1946 • PLAYED FOR TEAM: 1969 TO 1981

Ron Yary was one of the most *durable* players in team history. From 1970 to 1981, he missed only two games. During that time, Yary was an All-Pro six times.

CHUCK FOREMAN Running Back

- BORN: 10/26/1950 • PLAYED FOR TEAM: 1973 TO 1979

Chuck Foreman was a hardworking runner who did it all for the Vikings. Three times, he topped 1,000 yards on the ground. In 1975, he led the NFL with 73 catches, which set a record for running backs. Foreman played in the Pro Bowl five times.

LEFT: Fran Tarkenton   **ABOVE**: Ron Yary

MATT BLAIR Linebacker

- BORN: 9/20/1950 • PLAYED FOR TEAM: 1974 TO 1985

Matt Blair combined great speed and perfect timing to make plays all over the field. He had a special knack for batting away passes and blocking punts. Blair went to the Pro Bowl six years in a row with the Vikings.

RANDALL McDANIEL Offensive Lineman

- BORN: 12/19/1964 • PLAYED FOR TEAM: 1988 TO 1999

Randall McDaniel had quick feet for a big man. He was most dangerous "pulling" from the line and leading the way for running plays to the outside.

McDaniel teamed up with Gary Zimmerman to give Minnesota a great running attack.

JOHN RANDLE Defensive Lineman

- BORN: 12/12/1967
- PLAYED FOR TEAM: 1990 TO 2000

John Randle inspired his teammates with his hard work and high energy. He also continued Minnesota's *tradition* of great pass-rushers. In 11 seasons with the Vikings, he had 114 sacks.

CRIS CARTER Receiver

- BORN: 11/25/1965 • PLAYED FOR TEAM: 1990 TO 2001

Someone once criticized Cris Carter by saying all he did was "catch touchdown passes." Carter hauled in a lot of them, 110 in all for the Vikings. But he did much more than that. Carter was a good teammate and an even better leader.

RANDY MOSS   Receiver

• BORN: 2/13/1977   • PLAYED FOR TEAM: 1998 TO 2004

Randy Moss was a nightmare for opponents. He was big, fast, and almost impossible to stop on long passes. Moss was the Offensive Rookie of the Year in 1998 and led the NFL in touchdown catches three times with the Vikings.

ADRIAN PETERSON   Running Back

• BORN: 3/21/1985

• FIRST YEAR WITH TEAM: 2007

Adrian Peterson ran with a bruising style that left opponents limping to the sidelines. He created space where there seemed to be none and used his amazing speed to break away for long touchdowns. Peterson was the NFL's top rusher with 1,760 yards in 2008 and scored 18 touchdowns the following season.

JARED ALLEN   Defensive Lineman

• BORN: 4/3/1982

• FIRST YEAR WITH TEAM: 2008

When Jared Allen was traded to the Vikings, he fulfilled a dream that his father once had. Ron Allen had tried out for the Vikings in the 1980s, but the team cut him. His son made him proud. In 2011, Allen set a team record with 22 sacks.

LEFT: John Randle
RIGHT: Jared Allen

Calling the Shots

Picking the right coach for a new team can be very tricky. In 1961, the Vikings chose Norm Van Brocklin to lead the club. One season earlier, he had won the NFL title as the quarterback for the Philadelphia Eagles. Van Brocklin instantly earned the respect of the Minnesota players. He also got the fans excited about their new team.

One of Van Brocklin's goals was to build a strong defense. He also worked closely with young quarterback Fran Tarkenton. Like Van Brocklin, Tarkenton was very *competitive*, so the two did not always see eye to eye. After six seasons, the Vikings decided to make a change. They hired Bud Grant.

NFL fans knew little about Grant. He soon proved to be a great coach. In a span of eight seasons, he guided the Vikings to the Super Bowl four times. Throughout Grant's years with the Vikings, the team had an excellent defense. However, his greatest achievement may have come on the other side of the ball. Grant designed an offense that took advantage of the skills of his top players.

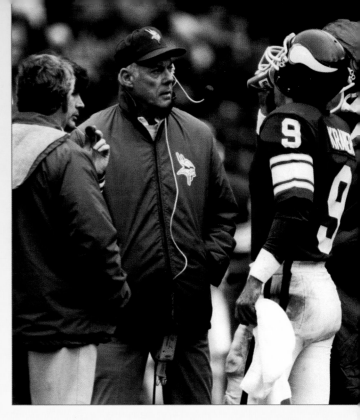

Bud Grant talks to quarterback Tommy Kramer during a timeout.

When Grant first joined the Vikings, he had two rugged running backs in Bill Brown and Dave Osborn. Minnesota wore down opponents with its rushing attack and only passed when necessary. Several years later, Grant turned the Vikings into a team that won with short passes. Their best running back, Chuck Foreman, ended up leading the league in receptions one year!

During the 1990s, Dennis Green used the same *strategy* to make the Vikings one of the top teams in football. He led Minnesota to the playoffs eight times in his first nine seasons. Green liked to use experienced quarterbacks who understood the ins and outs of his offense. Over the years, Rich Gannon, Jim McMahon, Warren Moon, Brad Johnson, Randall Cunningham, and Jeff George all had success with Minnesota. While other teams thought of these players as being "too old," Green found that they were a perfect fit with the Vikings.

One Great Day

It didn't take long for Minnesota fans to find out that Adrian Peterson was something special. Early in his rookie season in 2007, he broke the team's single-game rushing record with 224 yards against the Chicago Bears. Soon everyone understood why Peterson's nickname was "All Day"—hand him the ball, and he could run all day.

That's exactly what Peterson did against the San Diego Chargers later in his first year. When quarterback Tarvaris Jackson went down with an injury, Minnesota coach Brad Childress refocused his game plan. He called running plays for Peterson again and again. The strategy worked.

Peterson wore down the Chargers in the first two quarters and gained 43 yards. Hardly anyone noticed because San Diego's Antonio Cromartie returned a missed **field goal** 109 yards for a touchdown. It was the longest play in NFL history!

Minnesota fans put the squeeze on Adrian Peterson after a touchdown.

In the second half, Peterson decided to make some history of his own. He tore through the defense for touchdown runs of 46 yards and 64 yards. The Vikings led 35–17 with less than two minutes left. They handed the ball to Peterson so he could run out the clock. Amazingly, he broke off another long run of 35 yards—and almost went all the way for a 90-yard touchdown!

Peterson now had 293 yards for the day. That was just two yards short of the NFL record set in 2003 by Jamal Lewis of the Baltimore Ravens. The Vikings gave Peterson the ball one more time, and he gained three yards. That put his total at 296 yards for the game. Peterson broke the record!

Legend Has It

Did a knee injury help Randall McDaniel become an All-Pro?

LEGEND HAS IT that it did. After hurting his left knee early in his career, McDaniel was not able to bend it well enough to crouch down in his stance at the line of scrimmage. Instead, he stuck his left leg out to the side. This confused pass-rushers on the other side of the line. Even after his knee healed, McDaniel continued to use this stance. It helped him become one of the best blockers in history.

ABOVE: Randall McDaniel

Which Viking was famous for a scoreless season?

LEGEND HAS IT that Steve Jordan was. Jordan played tight end for Minnesota during the 1980s and 1990s. Because of his size and good hands, he was usually a reliable target near the end zone. But that wasn't the case in 1985. Jordan led the Vikings with 68 catches that season—by far the most of his career. However, not one of Jordan's catches came in the end zone. To this day, his season looks like a misprint: 16 games, 68 receptions, 795 yards, and zero touchdowns.

Which Viking made the most headlines off the field?

LEGEND HAS IT that Jim Marshall did. Once, he took a *stockbroker* test and scored at a genius level. Another time, he decided to go into the women's wig business. One winter, he took a daring snowmobile trip through the Grand Teton Mountains. Marshall also ended up in the hospital a lot. Once, he had an emergency *tonsillectomy* while visiting soldiers in Vietnam. Another time during summer training camp, a grape got stuck in his windpipe and he almost died.

It Really Happened

Jim Marshall enjoyed a lot of great moments during his 19 seasons with the Vikings. During the 1960s and 1970s, he was one of the best defensive linemen in football. Marshall almost never made a mistake. Unfortunately, the play that most people remember him for was one of the biggest mistakes in NFL history.

In the fall of 1964, the Vikings were playing the San Francisco 49ers. In a game one year earlier, Marshall had a big day against the 49ers. On one play, he picked up a San Francisco fumble and ran into the end zone for a touchdown.

Now Marshall had a chance to do it again. The Vikings stopped the 49ers after a short pass, and the ball popped loose. Marshall had been chasing the quarterback. When he saw the fumble, he reached the ball before anyone else. Marshall scooped it up and started running toward the end zone—except it was the wrong one!

Marshall rumbled 66 yards, crossed the goal line, and flung the ball in celebration. He thought he had just scored a touchdown, only to learn that he had actually been charged with a safety. When the

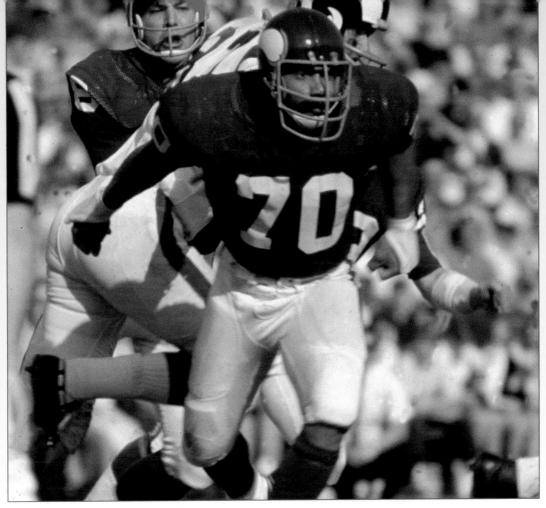

Jim Marshall recovered 30 fumbles during his career, but he is remembered for only one.

Vikings held on for a 27–22 victory, Marshall was the happiest man on the team.

Several weeks later, Marshall received a letter from Roy Riegels. He had made a similar wrong-way run decades earlier during an important college football game. The message from Riegels to Marshall was short and to the point: "Welcome to the club!"

Fans in Minnesota are some of the toughest in the NFL. When the team played in Metropolitan Stadium, they showed up to games in full force no matter how bad the weather got. The thermometer rarely climbed above 32 degrees during the last two months of the season, but that didn't bother the Vikings or their fans.

When the team moved into the Metrodome, the fans discovered a new home-field advantage. They filled the stadium with deafening noise at crucial points of games, making it difficult for opponents to concentrate. The Vikings were hard to beat in the Metrodome, and the crowd was a big reason why.

Minnesota fans also have fun **mascots** to help them cheer on the team. Viktor the Viking is a cartoon-style mascot who roams the sidelines during games. Ragnar is a real person dressed in Viking clothing. He is famous for shaving his beard with an axe!

LEFT: These fans show why the Vikings have one of the coolest team names in sports.   **ABOVE:** This pin was sold at the stadium in 1961, the team's first season.

n this timeline, each Super Bowl is listed under the year it was played. Remember that the Super Bowl is held early in the year and is actually part of the previous season. For example, Super Bowl XLVI was played on February 5, 2012, but it was the championship of the 2011 NFL season.

1961
The Vikings play their first season.

1970
The Vikings play in Super Bowl IV.

1965
Fred Cox leads the NFL in field goals.

1969
Joe Kapp throws seven touchdown passes in a game.

1981
Tommy Kramer leads the NFC in passing yards.

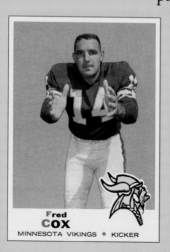

Fred Cox

Tommy Kramer

Chris
Doleman

Robert
Smith

1989
Chris Doleman leads
the NFL with 21 sacks.

2000
Robert Smith leads
the NFC in rushing.

2008
Adrian Peterson is
named All-Pro.

1994
Fuad Reveiz leads the
NFL in field goals.

1998
Randall Cunningham
is named NFL Player
of the Year.

2011
Percy Harvin scores
on a kickoff return
for the fourth time
in his career.

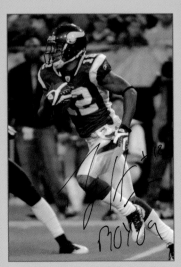

Percy
Harvin

Fun Facts

CATCHY TITLE

In 1994, NFL defenses simply could not handle the Minnesota passing attack. Jake Reed caught 84 passes, and Cris Carter caught 123. Their 207 receptions set a record that season. Later they became the first teammates to each have 1,000 receiving yards four years in a row.

SWISH!

Bud Grant coached the Vikings for 18 years, but he started his career in another sport. For two years, Grant played professional basketball for the Minneapolis Lakers. They won the championship in 1950.

LATE BLOOMER

Tommy Kramer's talent for winning games in the final moments earned him the nickname "Two-Minute Tommy." In 1980, his last-second touchdown bomb to Ahmad Rashad got the Vikings into the playoffs.

HERE COMES THE JUDGE

Alan Page spent 12 seasons chasing down quarterbacks for the Vikings. After he retired, he found a new line of work. Page was elected to serve as a judge on the Minnesota *Supreme Court*.

ALAN PAGE

DEFENSIVE TACKLE
VIKINGS

THANKS, BUT NO THANKS

After winning the NFL title in 1969, the Vikings voted quarterback Joe Kapp their team MVP. He refused the award because he felt Minnesota's success was a team effort. "I didn't want the honor," Kapp remembers. "To me, it didn't tell the truth."

FOOT NOTE

While growing up in South Africa, Gary Anderson hoped to become a pro soccer player. Three days after his family moved to America, he tried kicking a football for the first time. After 25 years in the NFL, he retired as the league's all-time scoring champion. In 1998, he didn't miss a kick during the regular season for the Vikings.

ABOVE: Alan Page

Talking Football

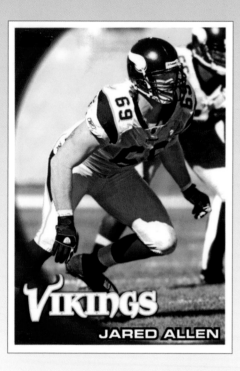

VIKINGS
JARED ALLEN

"I knew I could play. I knew I was going to be fine. I just kept my head up."

▶ **Jared Allen,** *on becoming a star after getting off to a slow start*

"He's the most important Viking of all. He took us from a struggling, struggling team to a very rock-solid football team."

▶ **Fran Tarkenton,** *on Bud Grant*

"The quarterback is the most *vulnerable* one on the field. He's in an awkward position a lot of times when he throws the ball."

▶ **Bud Grant,** *on the importance of protecting the passer*

"If I can get the ball in the open field, I can make a lot of things happen."

▶ **Percy Harvin,** *on his elusive running style*

"We knew we could count on Tommy. He got us going in the huddle."
► **Anthony Carter,** *on Tommy Kramer*

"I'm one of the most competitive guys in the NFL. Believe me, nobody wants it more than me."
► **Randy Moss,** *on playing to win*

"I dedicate myself and work hard in the weight room and treat every practice as if it were a game."
► **Adrian Peterson,** *on being prepared for kickoff each Sunday*

LEFT: Jared Allen
ABOVE: Anthony Carter

Great Debates

People who root for the Vikings love to compare their favorite moments, teams, and players. Some debates have been going on for years! How would you settle these classic football arguments?

Adrian Peterson is Minnesota's greatest runner ....

… because of his combination of size and speed. When Peterson (LEFT) first joined the Vikings, a lot of opponents underestimated him. They lined him up for easy tackles only to have him blow right past them. Those who tried to stop Peterson head-on often found themselves flat on their backs. In his first five seasons with the Vikings, he ran for more than 6,500 yards and scored a total of 67 touchdowns.

This one's not even close. Chuck Foreman wins this argument ....

… because he had more skills than any runner in the NFL. Foreman combined speed and power like Peterson, but he also had incredible moves. The first tackler almost always missed him. When Foreman wasn't running the ball, he was catching it. Don't forget that Foreman also led the Vikings to the Super Bowl three times.

The Vikings became a truly great team once they began playing indoors at the Metrodome ....

... because talented receivers such as the pass-catching trio (RIGHT) of Randy Moss, Cris Carter, and Jake Reed could show off their skills without worrying about cold weather and swirling winds. Experienced quarterbacks such as Rich Gannon and Warren Moon could handle the ball with confidence. The Metrodome gave Minnesota's most explosive players a chance to shine.

Indoor football may be great for the fans, but the Vikings were at their best playing outdoors ....

... because wind and ice and snow gave them a great home-field advantage. When the temperature dropped in Minnesota, no one wanted to go north and play the Vikings. Many opponents psyched themselves out before they left the locker room. That was especially true for quarterbacks. It was no fun getting tackled by Carl Eller and Alan Page on a frozen field.

For the Record

T he great Vikings teams and players have left their marks on the record books. These are the "best of the best" …

Chuck Foreman

Randy Moss

VIKINGS AWARD WINNERS

Paul Flatley	Rookie of the Year	1963
Fran Tarkenton	Pro Bowl co-MVP	1965
Bud Grant	Coach of the Year	1969
Alan Page	Defensive Player of the Year	1971
Alan Page	Most Valuable Player	1971
Chuck Foreman	Offensive Rookie of the Year	1973
Fran Tarkenton	Offensive Player of the Year	1975
Fran Tarkenton	Most Valuable Player	1975
Sammy White	Offensive Rookie of the Year	1976
Ahmad Rashad	Pro Bowl MVP	1979
Tommy Kramer	co-Comeback Player of the Year	1986
Keith Millard	Defensive Player of the Year	1989
Randy Moss	Offensive Rookie of the Year	1998
Randy Moss	Pro Bowl MVP	2000
Adrian Peterson	Offensive Rookie of the Year	2007
Adrian Peterson	Pro Bowl MVP	2008
Percy Harvin	Offensive Rookie of the Year	2009

VIKINGS ACHIEVEMENTS

ACHIEVEMENT	YEAR
Central Division Champions	1968
Central Division Champions	1969
NFL Champions	1969
NFC Central Champions	1970
NFC Central Champions	1971
NFC Central Champions	1973
NFC Champions	1973
NFC Central Champions	1974
NFC Champions	1974
NFC Central Champions	1975
NFC Champions	1976
NFC Central Champions	1976
NFC Central Champions	1977
NFC Central Champions	1978
NFC Central Champions	1980
NFC Central Champions	1989
NFC Central Champions	1992
NFC Central Champions	1994
NFC Central Champions	1998
NFC Central Champions	2000
NFC North Champions	2008
NFC North Champions	2009

TOP: Sammie White was Rookie of the Year in 1976. **RIGHT**: Brett Favre led the Vikings to the NFC title game in 2009.

Pinpoints

The history of a football team is made up of many smaller stories. These stories take place all over the map—not just in the city a team calls "home." Match the pushpins on these maps to the **Team Facts**, and you will begin to see the story of the Vikings unfold!

TEAM FACTS

1. Minneapolis, Minnesota—*The team has played in the Bloomington-Minneapolis area since 1961.*
2. Flint, Michigan—*Paul Krause was born here.*
3. Canton, Ohio—*Alan Page was born here.*
4. Ocala, Florida—*Daunte Culpepper was born here.*
5. Monongahela, Pennsylvania—*Fred Cox was born here.*
6. Danville, Kentucky—*Jim Marshall was born here.*
7. Portland, Oregon—*Ahmad Rashad was born here.*
8. Los Gatos, California—*Jared Allen was born here.*
9. Houston, Texas—*The Vikings played in Super Bowl VIII here.*
10. New Orleans, Louisiana—*The Vikings played in Super Bowl IV here.*
11. Parys, South Africa—*Gary Anderson was born here.*
12. Bogota, Colombia—*Fuad Reveiz was born here.*

Ahmad Rashad

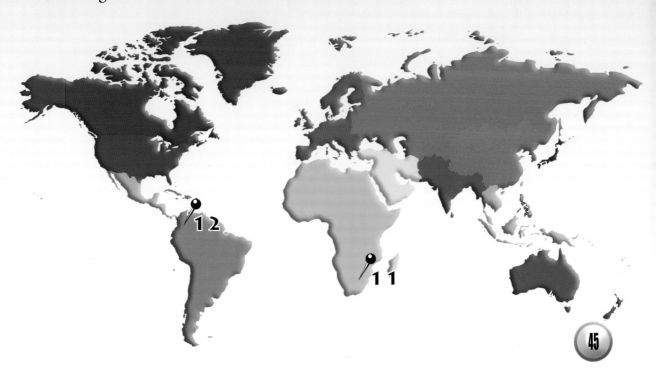

Glossary

🏈 **Football Words**
📖 **Vocabulary Words**

🏈 **ALL-PRO**—An honor given to the best players at their positions at the end of each season.

🏈 **AMERICAN FOOTBALL LEAGUE (AFL)**—The football league that began play in 1960 and later merged with the NFL.

📖 **ANCHORED**—Held steady.

🏈 **CANADIAN FOOTBALL LEAGUE (CFL)**—A professional league in Canada that began play in 1958.

📖 **COMPETITIVE**—Having a strong desire to win.

📖 **DECADE**—A period of 10 years; also specific periods, such as the 1950s.

📖 **DURABLE**—Able to avoid or withstand injury.

📖 **ERA**—A period of time in history.

🏈 **EXTRA POINT**—A kick worth one point, attempted after a touchdown.

🏈 **FIELD GOAL**—A goal from the field, kicked over the crossbar and between the goal posts. A field goal is worth three points.

🏈 **FUMBLE**—A ball that is dropped by the player carrying it.

🏈 **INTERCEPT**—Caught in the air by a defensive player.

🏈 **LINE OF SCRIMMAGE**—The imaginary line that separates the offense and defense before each play begins.

📖 **LOGO**—A symbol or design that represents a company or team.

📖 **MASCOTS**—Animals or people believed to bring a group good luck.

🏈 **MOST VALUABLE PLAYER (MVP)**—The award given each year to the league's best player; also given to the best player in the Super Bowl and Pro Bowl.

🏈 **NATIONAL FOOTBALL CONFERENCE (NFC)**—One of two groups of teams that make up the NFL.

🏈 **NATIONAL FOOTBALL LEAGUE (NFL)**—The league that started in 1920 and is still operating today.

🏈 **NFL CHAMPIONSHIP GAME**—The game played to decide the winner of the league each year from 1933 to 1969.

🏈 **OVERTIME**—The extra period played when a game is tied after 60 minutes.

🏈 **PLAYOFFS**—The games played after the regular season to determine which teams play in the Super Bowl.

🏈 **PRO BOWL**—The NFL's all-star game, played after the regular season.

📖 **PROFESSIONAL**—Paid to play.

🏈 **ROOKIE**—A player in his first season.

🏈 **SACKS**—Tackles of the quarterback behind the line of scrimmage.

🏈 **SAFETY**—A tackle of a ball carrier in his own end zone. A safety is worth two points.

🏈 **SECONDARY**—The part of the defense made up by the cornerbacks and safeties.

📖 **STOCKBROKER**—Someone who buys and sells shares of a business.

📖 **STRATEGY**—A plan or method for succeeding.

🏈 **SUPER BOWL**—The championship of the NFL, played between the winners of the National Football Conference and American Football Conference.

📖 **SUPREME COURT**—The highest court in a state.

📖 **TONSILLECTOMY**—An operation to remove the tonsils.

📖 **TRADITION**—A belief or custom that is handed down from generation to generation.

📖 **UNDERESTIMATED**—Placed too low a value on.

📖 **VULNERABLE**—Open to attack or injury.

🏈 **WESTERN CONFERENCE**—A group of teams that play in the western part of the country.

OVERTIME

TEAM SPIRIT introduces a great way to stay up to date with your team! Visit our **OVERTIME** link and get connected to the latest and greatest updates. **OVERTIME** serves as a young reader's ticket to an exclusive web page—with more stories, fun facts, team records, and photos of the Vikings. Content is updated during and after each season. The **OVERTIME** feature also enables readers to send comments and letters to the author! Log onto:

www.norwoodhousepress.com/library.aspx

and click on the tab: **TEAM SPIRIT** to access **OVERTIME**.

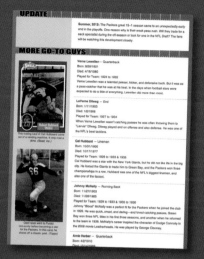

Read all the books in the series to learn more about professional sports. For a complete listing of the baseball, basketball, football, and hockey teams in the **TEAM SPIRIT** series, visit our website at:

www.norwoodhousepress.com/library.aspx

On the Road

MINNESOTA VIKINGS
900 South 5th Street
Minneapolis, Minnesota 55415
952-828-6500
www.vikings.com

THE PRO FOOTBALL HALL OF FAME
2121 George Halas Drive NW
Canton, Ohio 44708
330-456-8207
www.profootballhof.com

On the Bookshelf

To learn more about the sport of football, look for these books at your library or bookstore:

* Frederick, Shane. *The Best of Everything Football Book.* North Mankato, Minnesota: Capstone Press, 2011.

* Jacobs, Greg. *The Everything Kids' Football Book: The All-Time Greats, Legendary Teams, Today's Superstars—And Tips on Playing Like a Pro.* Avon, Massachusetts: Adams Media Corporation, 2010.

* Editors of *Sports Illustrated for Kids. 1st and 10: Top 10 Lists of Everything in Football.* New York, New York: Sports Illustrated Books, 2011.

Index

PAGE NUMBERS IN **BOLD** REFER TO ILLUSTRATIONS.

About the Author

MARK STEWART has written more than 50 books on football and over 150 sports books for kids. He grew up in New York City during the 1960s rooting for the Giants and Jets, and was lucky enough to meet players from both teams. Mark comes from a family of writers. His grandfather was Sunday Editor of *The New York Times,* and his mother was Articles Editor of *Ladies' Home Journal* and *McCall's.* Mark has profiled hundreds of athletes over the past 25 years. He has also written several books about his native New York and New Jersey, his home today. Mark is a graduate of Duke University, with a degree in history. He lives and works in a home overlooking Sandy Hook, New Jersey. You can contact Mark through the Norwood House Press website.